Bitcoin

The Definite Guide to the World of Cryptocurrency

(for Business, Engineering, Investing, Mining, Trading and more)

Richard Brana

Copyright © 2017 Richard Brana

All rights reserved.

Table of Contents

Introduction 5

Chapter One – The History and Future of Bitcoins 7

Chapter Two - Understanding Bitcoin Transactions 13
    So how does a transaction work? 14
    How are they sent? 14
    Why do I have to wait for a transaction to clear? 14
    What if the input and output amounts don't match up? 15
    Are there transaction fees? 16
    Can I obtain a receipt? 16
    What if I only want to send part of a Bitcoin? 16

Chapter Three - How to Get Bitcoins 17
    #1 Obtain a Mining Rig 17
    #2 Obtain a Bitcoin Wallet 18
    #3 Find a Mining Pool 18
    #4 Obtain a Mining Program 19
    #5 Begin Mining 20

Chapter Four - How to Keep and Spend Bitcoins 21

Chapter Five - Bitcoins for Engineers 24
    Mining Difficulty 24
    Mining Hardware 25
    Mining Pools 25
    Costs to Consider 26
    Regulations 26

Chapter Six - Bitcoins for Investors 28
    Other Ways to Purchase 29

Chapter Seven - Bitcoins for Business 30
    Why Companies Should Use Bitcoins 30
    Countries that Accept Bitcoin 34
    Countries that Do Not Accept Bitcoins 36

Chapter Eight - Bitcoins for Regular Non-Technical Users 37

Chapter Nine - Bitcoin Wallets 40
    Universal Wallets 41
    Hardware Wallets 41
    Online Bitcoin Wallets 42
    Mobile Wallets for Android 43
    Mobile Wallets for iOS 43

    Desktop Wallets..43
    Paper Wallets..44
Chapter Ten - Important Warnings about Bitcoins..................45

Chapter Eleven - Short Guide on Other Cryptocurrencies......48

    #1 Litecoin..48
    #2 Ethereum 49
    #3 Zcash 49
    #4 Dash 50
    #5 Ripple 50
    #6 Monero 50
Conclusion 52

Bonus: Fun Facts about Bitcoins 53

Introduction

Created in 2008, Bitcoin is a cryptocurrency originating from an unknown source with the alias Satoshi Nakamoto. The platform for Bitcoin allows you to make transactions without a middleman online, which means no banks, no fees, and no ability to trace who sent what where. There's no need to use your real name, and more merchants are starting to accept them across the globe. You can purchase a web hosting service, order pizza, or pay for your next manicure with a Bitcoin.

Bitcoins are able to be used to purchase anything anonymously, and international payments are simple and low-cost because the Bitcoins aren't tied to a country or subject to any regulations. Small businesses like them because they don't need to pay a fee to credit card companies. Some people just purchase them as an investment because the value may continue to increase.

There are a few different ways you can obtain a Bitcoin, which we'll go over in more detail in later chapters. You can purchase them on an online marketplace, known as a Bitcoin exchange, which allows you to purchase or sell Bitcoins using almost any currency. The largest Bitcoin exchange today is Mt. Gox. Another way to receive a Bitcoin is through a transfer.

People are transferring them through a mobile application or their computers. It's a lot like sending cash digitally.

You can find them through mining by competing with others using your computer to solve a complex math equation. This is how a Bitcoin is made. Currently, winners are rewarded with twenty-five Bitcoins about every ten minutes.

When you own a Bitcoin, you can store them in a digital wallet, which can be in the cloud or on your computer. The wallet's a lot like a virtual bank account that lets you send or receive a Bitcoin, pay for services or goods, or save your money. Unlike a bank account, a Bitcoin wallet is not insured by the FDIC. Therefore, you need to make sure your wallet is in a secure location. We'll talk more about that in this book.

While every Bitcoin transaction is logged in a public log, the names of the sellers and buyers are never exposed. Only your wallet ID is public. While that keeps your transactions private, it lets you purchase or sell anything without having someone trace it back to you. Therefore, the Bitcoin has obtained a bad reputation for being a breeding ground for money laundering.

This last fact has led some to believe the Bitcoin will not be around forever, but while it's mostly not regulated now, that fact might change in the future. Governments are concerned about being able to control their currency and tax income, and once Bitcoins are entangled in the government, they could be here to stay.

Therefore, it's a good idea to learn about and potentially invest in Bitcoins now before they become too main stream. Who knows, Bitcoins could be the next big thing when it comes to investing, and you can get ahead of the game!

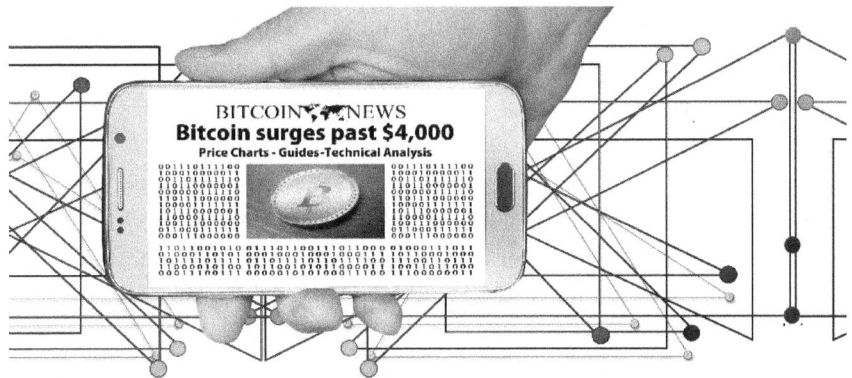

Chapter One – The History and Future of Bitcoins

Since October of 2008, the adoption of Bitcoins has been influenced by many different factors. These have made it one of the most volatile currencies across the globe. However, despite this volatility, more than a hundred thousand Bitcoin transactions happen each day, and the volume is continuing to grow because of the freedom of the blockchain.

While the blockchain grows, the Bitcoin is going to grow into resembling a traditional financial institution equipped with retail banking, exchanges, and payment processors. But how did this all begin, and where is it going? Here, we're going to take a brief look at the major milestones of this cryptocurrency, and take a look at where it might lead.

In August of 2008, three people – Vladimir Oksman, Neal Kin, and Charles Bry – filed an application for an encryption patent. All three of these people have denied having a connection to Satoshi Nakamoto, who is the public originator of the Bitcoin idea. The three registered the site Bitcoin.org the same month, on the anonymousspeech.com website. This site lets people purchase domain names without identification.

In October of 2008, Satoshi Nakamoto published his white paper, which revealed his idea for a peer-to-peer version of virtual cash. In this vision, he managed to solve the issue of money being copied, which is the basis Bitcoin grew from.

In January of 2009, the first black, Genesis, was launched to let the first mining of Bitcoins begin. Later on that month, the first transaction took place between Hal Finney and Satoshi, a developer and a cryptographic activist.

In October of that same year, Bitcoin received an equivalent value in traditional currencies. A Bitcoin value of $1 equaling 1,309 BTC was established by the New Liberty Standard. The equation was created so as to include the cost of electricity to run the equipment needed to make a Bitcoin in the first place.

In February of 2010, the first Bitcoin market was created by the now defunct dwdollar.

In May of 2010, a programmer who lived in Florida and went by the name of Laslo Hanyecz sent 10,000 BTC to a volunteer in England, who spent around $25 to order Hanyecz a pizza from a Papa John's. That pizza would be valued at £1,961,034 and was a major landmark in Bitcoin's past.

In August of that same year, Bitcoin was hacked. This vulnerability in the system that verified how a Bitcoin was valued was found, which led to the generation of 184 billion Bitcoins. The value of the currency, which had gone from eighty cents to a dollar in June, plummeted.

Two months later, in October, Bitcoin was in the spotlight. After they were hacked in August, and more discoveries of vulnerabilities in the blockchain were unearthed in September, an inter-governmental group published a report on money launder using new payment methods. This report suggested Bitcoin could finance terrorist groups.

In November of 2010, Bitcoin reached one million dollars. Based on the number that was in circulation at the time, the valuation led to a surge in Bitcoin value of $0.50 per Bitcoin.

In January of 2011, The Silk Road, a drug marketplace, was created. They used Bitcoin as an undetectable way to purchase and sell drugs on the internet. February of that year, Bitcoin reached parity with the US dollar for the first time in its history. By June, every Bitcoin was worth $31, which gave the currency a market cap of $206 million.

In June of 2013, the first major theft happened. The Bitcoin forum founder allinvain reported having 25,000 BTC stolen from his digital wallet, which was the equivalent value of $375,000. That same month, a major breach of the security saw the value of the currency go from $17.51 to $0.01 per Bitcoin. March of that same year, the US Financial Crimes Enforcement Network issued some of the world's first regulations on Bitcoins in the forms of guidance report for people administering, exchanging, or using the virtual currency. This started the beginning of an ongoing debate on how to regulate Bitcoins. The Bitcoin market capitalization reached $1 billion that same month.

In August of 2013, a federal judge claimed it was clear that Bitcoin could be used as money, and it was able to be used to purchase goods and services. Bloomberg started testing Bitcoin on its terminal. While alternative tickers are out there, endorsement from Bloomberg gave Bitcoin more institutional legitimacy.

November of 2013, the Bitcoin price climbed to $700. The United States Senate held its first hearing on the currency. Ben Bernanke, the Federal Reserve Chairman, gave his blessing to the new digital currency. In his letter to the Senate, Homeland Security, and Government Affairs Committee, he stated that Bitcoin might hold long-term promise, especially if the innovates encouraged a quicker, more secure, and more efficient payment system. December of that year, China barred financial institutions from handling the transactions. This ban was enacted after the People's Bank of Chain said Bitcoin wasn't a currency with real meaning, and it didn't have the same legal status as sanctioned legal tender. The ban reflected the risk Bitcoin posed to China's capital controls and their financial stability. Today, China is the world's largest Bitcoin trader, with eighty percent of the world's Bitcoin trades being handled in China.

January of 2014, Elliptic, Bitcoin custodians, launched the world's first insured storage device for Bitcoins for institutional clients. All deposits are insured by the Fortune 100 insurer and held in full reserve. This means that they never reinvest client assets. Rather, they secure them in deep, cold storage. Overstock.com was the first main online shop to accept Bitcoin, accepting payments in the United States. They were the first in what is now a rapidly growing list of large businesses that accept this cryptocurrency.

In February of 2014, HMRC classified Bitcoin as an asset or private money, meaning no VAT would be charged on the mining or exchange of Bitcoin. This is important because it's the world's first and most progressive treatment of Bitcoins, positioning the United Kingdom government as the most progressive and comprehensive with regards to Bitcoin taxation.

In June of that same year, the United States government auctioned off more than 29,000 Bitcoins that were seized from the Silk Road, the illegal online marketplace that sold illegal drugs and paraphernalia. The sale and closure of the marketplace marked a growing institutional understanding of the potential use cases of Bitcoin. In addition, the closure and auction of The Silk Road helped Bitcoin gain legitimacy as it demonstrated that Bitcoin wasn't an easy way for online criminals to avoid the laws.

From this point forward, Bitcoin was no longer considered a currency for criminals. The use of the Bitcoin blockchain meant that the identity of the users was able to be established.

In July of 2014, the Bit License edged toward reality as the New York State Department of Financial Services released the first draft of their proposed rules pertaining to regulating virtual currencies. Their report recommended that the European Union legislators consider declaring virtual currency marketplaces as obliged entities, and so they must comply with anti-money laundering and counter-terrorist financing regulations.

The EBA report was important because it acted as a facilitator to liftoff Bitcoin into the mainstream through highlighting the truth that virtual exchanges need a supervisory approach.

In this month, Global Advisors Bitcoin Investment Fund backed the world's first controlled Bitcoin investment fund. This was an important stepping stone to the Bitcoin market because the launch of this investment method added a further legitimacy to Bitcoin, in addition to letting regulated investors a way to invest in Bitcoin.

In August of that same year, George Osborne, the Chancellor of the Exchequer, demonstrated HM Treasury's and his positive opinion of Bitcoin's future when he purchased £20 worth of Bitcoins and announced HM Treasury's call for information on digital currencies. This offered digital currency businesses the opportunity to comment on the risks and benefits, as well as the potential influence of government policy in the future.

In October of 2014, TeraExchange announced the first Bitcoin derivative transaction had been performed on a controlled exchange. This added a new dodging tool to Bitcoin and instilled institutional confidence and credibility in the Bitcoin community.

December of that year, Microsoft started accepting Bitcoin payments.

January of the following year, 2015, the NY Stock Exchange became a minor investor in Coinbase's $75 million funding round. The NYSE aimed to tap into the new asset class by bringing security, transparency, and confidence to Bitcoin.

March of that year, the results of the UK Treasury's call for information on digital currency was released.

There are a few ways Bitcoin can go from here, all of which are pointing in the direction of a genuine, extensive adoption by large banking institutions through tighter regulations. Recently, BitLicense became the world's first digital currency-specific regulatory company. It's been through a few rounds of constitutions.

The European Banking author and European Central Bank both released detailed reports on cryptocurrencies and suggested regulation of the industry by the European Union to control the price fluctuations.

Bitcoin's expedition into the financial mainstream has begun.

Chapter Two - Understanding Bitcoin Transactions

The first thing you need to know about Bitcoins is there are no Bitcoins. There are only the records of Bitcoin transactions. It sounds like something out of a science-fiction or futuristic film, but it's reality right now, right here. Bitcoins don't exist, and yet, they are being used as a currency.

Bitcoins don't exist anywhere, not even in on a hard drive. They are talked about as if someone has a Bitcoin, but when you look at the specific address, there are no digital Bitcoins held in that address like you would hold dollars in a bank account. You can't pinpoint the physical object, or even point toward a digital file, and say it's a Bitcoin.

Instead, there are just the records of the transactions between the different addresses. There are balances that decrease and increase at those addresses. Every transaction that has ever taken place is stored in a public ledger known as a block chain. If you want to figure out the balance of a Bitcoin address, the information isn't at that address. You have to reconstruct it through looking at the blockchain.

So how does a transaction work?

If John sends Bitcoins to Jane, then that transaction will have three imperative pieces of data. First, it will have an input. This is the recording of what Bitcoin address was used in order to send the Bitcoins to John, to begin with. He may have received them from his friend, Bob. The third piece of information is the amount. This is the amount that John is sending to Jane. The final piece of information is the output. This is Jane's Bitcoin address.

How are they sent?

In order to send a Bitcoin to your friend, you need two things – their address and a private key. Bitcoin addresses are generated at random, and they are a sequence of letters and numbers. The private key is a separate sequence of letters and numbers, but unlike the address, the private key is secret.

Think of the Bitcoin address as a safety deposit box with a glass front. Everyone knows what's in there, but only the private key is able to unlock it to take out the contents or put something in.

When John sends a Bitcoin to Jane, he uses his private key to sign a message with the input, which is the source transaction of the coin, amount, and the output discussed in the previous section.

Joh then sends them from his Bitcoin wallet to the larger Bitcoin network. After that, the Bitcoin miners confirm the deal, which puts it into a transaction block and eventually solves it.

Why do I have to wait for a transaction to clear?

The transaction has to be verified by miners, so sometimes you have to wait until they've finished mining. The Bitcoin protocol is setup so that every block takes about ten minutes to mine.

Some merchants might make you wait until the block has been

confirmed, which means you might need to make a cup of tea and come back again in a bit before you can download the Bitcoin or take advantage of a paid service.

However, there are some merchants that won't make you wait until the transaction has been confirmed. Effectively, they're taking a chance on you and assuming that you're not trying to use the same Bitcoins someplace else before the operation has been confirmed. This happens for a low-value transaction, where the risk of fraud isn't so great.

What if the input and output amounts don't match up?

Because a Bitcoin exists only as a record of a transaction, you can end up with a few different transactions tied to one Bitcoin address. Maybe John sent Jane two Bitcoins, Bob sent he three, and Alice sent her one Bitcoin, all as a separate transaction at different times.

These aren't automatically combined in Jane's wallet to make a single file with six Bitcoins. They'll all be there with different transaction records.

When John wants to send Bitcoins to Jane, his wallet is going to try to use transaction records that have different amounts that add up to the number of Bitcoins he wants to send to her. Odds are, when John wants to send Bitcoins to Jane, he won't have the right number of Bitcoins from the other transactions. Maybe he only wants to send 2.5 BTC to Jane.

None of the transactions he has in his Bitcoin address are for that specific amount, and none of them add up to that amount when they're combined. John can't just split a transaction into a smaller amount. He can only spend the entire output of a transaction, instead of breaking it up into smaller amounts.

Instead, he has to send one of the incoming transactions, and then the rest of the Bitcoins will be returned to him as change.

John sends the three Bitcoins he received from Karl to Jane. Karl is the input, and Jane is the output. However, the amount is only 2.5 BTC because that's all he wants to send. Therefore, his wallet automatically makes two outputs for the transaction, 2.5 BTC to Jane, and 0.5 BTC to a new address, which is made for John to hold his change from Jane.

Are there transaction fees?

Some marketplaces charge a transaction fee, but not all of them do. These are calculated by many different factors. Some wallets will let you set a transaction fee manually. Any portion of the transaction not picked up by the receiver or refunded as change is a fee. This goes to the miner who is lucky enough to solve the transaction as an extra reward.

However, many miners process transactions without a fee. As the block prize for Bitcoins drops, this is going to be less likely in the future. One of the annoying things pertaining to transaction fees in history was that the calculation of them was complex. It's been the result of a few updates to the protocol and has developed naturally.

Core software updates to the software that handles the Bitcoin transactions will change how it handles transaction fees.

Can I obtain a receipt?

Originally, you couldn't obtain a receipt when you used a Bitcoin or received one, but there are some changes coming in the future that will alter how payments work, which makes them far more mature and user-friendly.
Payment processes, such as BitPay, provide the advanced features you wouldn't normally find with a native Bitcoin transaction.

What if I only want to send part of a Bitcoin?

A Bitcoin transaction is divisible. Satoshis are one hundred millionth of a Bitcoin, and it's possible to send transactions as small as 5,430 satoshis now.
Now that you know how transactions work in Bitcoin let's take a look at how to get them!

Chapter Three - How to Get Bitcoins

So now you're aware of how Bitcoins started, and how the transactions work, so how do you get them? There is one main way you can get Bitcoins, and that's by mining them. The other way is to purchase them, but that's not really profitable, is it? It's much better to setup a mining machine and hope you find a Bitcoin than to purchase them and potentially lose out.

So how do you get a mining rig going?

#1 Obtain a Mining Rig

Bitcoin mining is a competitive niche to enter into, and as more and more miners start setting up rigs with the newest mining hardware, the hardness of mining will increase each day. Before you even start out with Bitcoin mining, you have to do your research. This means you need to figure out if Bitcoin mining is going to be profitable for you.

The best way to do this is to find an online Bitcoin mining calculator. Plug in the information of the Bitcoin miner you want to use and figure out how long it'll take you to break even or make a profit. However, if you don't have a few hundred dollars you can spare on a machine, then you most likely won't be able to mine a Bitcoin.

Once you've finished your calculations, it's time to obtain a miner. Be sure to go over the Bitcoin mining hardware assessments online to figure out which miner is the best one for you.

Keep in mind that it was significant to say in the past that it was conceivable to mine Bitcoins with a personal computer or with a graphics card, which was known as GPU mining. However, today, the mining niche is so competitive that you need an ASIC miner. These are computers that are built specifically for mining Bitcoins.

#2 Obtain a Bitcoin Wallet

The first thing you need to get is a wallet and not one you put in your pocket. Due to Bitcoin being an internet based currency or a cryptocurrency, you have to have a place to keep them. Once you have a wallet, you need to get a wallet address. It'll be a long string of letters and numbers. Every wallet has a different way to get the public address, but most of them are pretty easy to use. Notice that you need a public Bitcoin address and not the private key, which is a password for the wallet.

If you're using a self-hosted wallet, such as you download a program to your computer and you're not using an internet based service, then there's another step that's imperative. Be sure you have a copy of the wallet.dat file on a separate device, such as a thumb drive, and print out a copy to keep in a fire proof box. The reason is if your computer crashes and you don't have a copy of your wallet.dat file, then you'll lose all the Bitcoins in your wallet. They won't go to someone else, but they'll disappear forever.

It would be like burning cash.

#3 Find a Mining Pool

Now that you've downloaded and installed a wallet, or you have one online, it's time to start making Bitcoin. You'll need to join a mining pool to do this. Mining pools are groups of Bitcoin users that combine their computing power to make a Bitcoin. The reason you don't want to go it alone is because Bitcoins are usually awarded in blocks around 12.5 at a time, and unless you're very lucky, you'll not obtain any of those coins.

In a pool, there are smaller and easier algorithms to solve, so all your combined work makes you more likely to solve a larger algorithm and earn a Bitcoin that is spread out throughout the pool based on the contribution you made. Basically, you make a more dependable quantity of Bitcoins and are more likely to receive a good return on your investment.

When you're looking for a mining pool to join, ask a few questions first.

1. What is the reward method? It is score based, proportional, pay per share or PPLNS.
2. What fee is charged for mining and for withdrawing your funds?
3. How frequently do they find a block?
4. What types of stats will they provide?
5. How easy is it for you to withdraw funds?
6. How stable is the pool?

Once you sign up with a pool, you get a username and password you can use later on.

Follow the link on the mining pool's site to sign up, and follow their instructions. After you've set up your account, you'll need to add a worker. This means that for every miner you have running, you need to have a worker ID, so the pool is able to keep track of what you contributed.

#4 Obtain a Mining Program

Now that you have the basics down, it's about time to mine. You'll need a mining client on your computer that you can use to control and monitor your mining setup. Depending on what mining rig you have, you'll need to find the proper software. Many mining pools have software they prefer you use, but some of them don't.

#5 Begin Mining

Alright, so now everything is ready to go. Connect the miner to the power outlet and turn it on. Make sure you connect it to your computer, via a USB port, and open up the mining software. The first thing you have to do is enter your mining pool's username and password.

Once this is setup, you'll start mining for the Bitcoins. You'll actually begin collections shares, which represent your chunk of the work for finding the next block. According to the pool you chose, you will be paid for your share of the coins. Just be sure you enter your address into the required fields when you sign up for the pool.

And that's how you start mining Bitcoins! Now, let's take a look at how you can keep and spend your Bitcoins.

Chapter Four - How to Keep and Spend Bitcoins

If you want to keep Bitcoins and spend them, then you need to have a Bitcoin wallet. We're going to go into more detail about specific wallets in a future chapter, but in this chapter, we'll take a look at the different *types* of wallets, and which ones you should use.

There is one basic rule to hanging onto your Bitcoins and keeping your wallet safe, and that's don't ever give someone your private key. This means you shouldn't use any of these types of wallets.

- Online web wallets, such as blockchain.info and Coinbase. Usually, all wallets that keep the private key on their servers are not a good idea.
- Hot wallets. Any app on your phone or computer that is used with an Internet connection is not a good idea. You can use them to store small amounts in order to make payments, but don't store your entire collection of Bitcoins on there.

If you want to keep your Bitcoins safe, you need to use cold storage. Cold storage, when it comes to Bitcoins, refers to keeping a reserve of them offline. Methods for keeping them in cold storage include:

- Using a USB drive or another storage media
- Keeping them in a paper wallet
- A bearer item, like a physical Bitcoin
- Or offline Bitcoin hardware wallets.

Here's one way to keep your Bitcoins safe.

1. **Make a bootable USB flash drive.**

Make a bootable USB flash drive that has permanent encrypted storage. One program to use is Tails because it has a Bitcoin wallet and encryption out of the box. Create two passwords – one for login and the other for encryption.

2. **Make a cold wallet.**

Boot up Tails without using the internet. Make your cold wallet using the program Electrum. Make a complex password by writing down twelve to thirteen seed words on paper. These twelve words should be used to make your password, which will allow you to access your wallet from any computer in the future.

You need to make sure you check the box next to the 'View Transaction Before Signing' option in the settings for your wallet. If you don't do this, Electrum will show the transaction details before you enter the password and send that transaction to the network.

3. **Make a 'watch-only' wallet in your cell phone or on your main operating system.**

Copy public address for the Bitcoin from Electrum into a text document on your USB drive and shut down Tails. Make a 'watch-only' wallet with the public address in the wallet app you choose on the main operating system or on a cell phone. Now, you can view the balance of your Bitcoins, but you can't spend them.

4. **Spend your Bitcoins safely.**

To send the Bitcoins safely, run the Tails program again without the internet. Then, make a transaction. When you do, a window will appear that will have you sign and enter your password. When you do, click the 'save' button. Don't send the transaction to the network, and be sure not to allow the internet to access it. Just copy that transaction file to a flash drive.

Start in the main operating system, open the wallet, and in the menu, choose the load transaction from file setting. Then, load the signed transaction from the flash drive and push the 'broadcast' button. This will send the signed transaction to the block chain from your 'watch-only' wallet, and the private key won't be leaked from the Tails USB.

It's important that you always check the address after you've copied it into the field.

Chapter Five - Bitcoins for Engineers

We talked about mining a little bit in a previous chapter, but we're going to go into it in more detail in this chapter. We'll explore topics such as how difficult it is to mine, hardware you need, mining pools, and expenses you should keep in mind.

Mining Difficulty

The mining difficulty of Bitcoins depends on how many other miners there are and how much power they're putting into mining at the time. Following the protocol in the software, the Bitcoin network will automatically adjust the difficulty of mining every 2,016 blocks, or about every two weeks. It will readjust with the goal of keeping the rate of discovering blocks constant. Therefore, if more computational power is used in the mining process, then the difficulty will adjust upward to make the mining more difficult. And if the computational power is taken off the network, then the opposite will occur. The difficulty will adjust downward to make the mining easier.

The harder it is, the less profitable the mining will be for the miners.

Therefore, the more people who are mining, the less profitable it will be for each individual. The total payout will depend on the price of the Bitcoin, the block reward, and the size of the transaction fees associated with the mining, but the more people who are mining, the smaller the percentage of the profit each person will receive.

Mining Hardware

Anyone who has an internet connection and the appropriate hardware can participate in mining Bitcoins. In the earlier days of the currency, mining was completed on CPUs from a normal desktop or laptop. Graphic processing units, or graphics cards, are better at mining than a CPU. As Bitcoin became more popular, GPUs were dominant in the mining industry.

Eventually, hardware known as Application-Specific Integrated Circuit, or ASIC, was designed with the sole purpose of mining Bitcoins. The first ones came about in 2013, and they have been improved upon since their release. There are now highly sophisticated, efficient design on the market today. Mining is so competitive now that it can only be done profitably with the latest ASICs. When you use a GPU, CPU, or an older ASIC, the cost of the energy you need to use in order to obtain a Bitcoin is greater than what the Bitcoin is worth.

As the ASICs advanced and more miners entered onto the scene, the difficulty shot up insanely. Most of this activity was incentivized by the Bitcoin's price increase it experienced in 2013, and speculations are out there that say the price will go higher. There's political power in the Bitcoin ecosystem when an individual controls the mining power because that mining power gives you a vote on whether to accept changes to the current protocol.

There are numerous companies out there that make ASICs, just be careful and do your research when you decide to purchase one.

Mining Pools

Mining prizes are rewarded to the miner who ascertains the answer to the problem first, and the probability that miner will be the one to discover the solution is equal to the amount of the total mining power that's on their network. Participants that have a small percentage of the mining power have a small chance of obtaining the next block alone. For example, a mining card you could purchase for a few thousand dollars would symbolize under a hundred of one percent of the network's mining power.

Since you have such a small chance of finding the next block, it might be a long time before you find one, and the difficulty going up makes it even harder. You might never recoup your investment. The answer to this problem is simple – mining pools. Mining pools are created by a third party, which is made up of a group of miners. By working together and sharing the spoils, miners get a steady flow of Bitcoin as soon as they activate their miner.

Costs to Consider

The main operational cost a miner has is the electricity they're using and the mining equipment they have to purchase. Not only do you have to worry about the electricity the mining equipment will use, but you also have to worry about cooling costs and ventilation costs. A miner can heat up a household pretty quickly! Some major mining operations are purposefully located near cheap electricity.

The largest mining operation in North America is run by MegaBigPower, and it's located by the Columbia River in Washington. Electricity prices are very low there due to hydroelectricity. CloudHashing has a large mining operation in Iceland. The electricity there is generated by geothermal power and hydroelectric power. These are both renewable and inexpensive, and the cold climate there provides the operations with inexpensive cooling.

Regulations

In the United States, the IRS has issued some tax guidelines regarding mining Bitcoins and has said that income from mining is considered self-employment income, which is subjected to self-employment taxes. The

Financial Crimes Enforcement Network is a bureau of the United States Treasury, and they collect and analyze data on financial transactions with the goal of fighting money laundering and terrorist financing. They have issued guidelines saying that Bitcoin miners aren't considered money transmitters under the Bank Secrecy Act, and just made clear that those who provide cloud mining services are not considered Money Transmitters.

In short, mining is the means by which a new Bitcoin is entered into circulation, and the total Bitcoins that will ever be brought into circulation is 21 million. Miners are racing each other to obtain these Bitcoins, and the difficulty is increasing exponentially because of their increase of power and the increase of miners.

Chapter Six - Bitcoins for Investors

The easiest way you can invest in Bitcoin is to outright purchase them. Buying Bitcoins today is easier than it ever was before. There are numerous established companies in the United States and in other countries that are involved in the business of purchasing and selling Bitcoins. For the investors in the United States, the easiest solution is a marketplace called Coinbase. This company sells Bitcoins to consumers at a markup that's around one percent over the current market value.

For those in the United States, Coinbase has the option to link your bank account to the Coinbase wallet. This makes future payments much simpler. The company offers an spontaneous Bitcoin purchasing at regular intermissions. As an example, let's say you'd like to purchase fifty dollars' worth of Bitcoins every first or second of the month, right after your paycheck is deposited. You can setup and auto-purchase for that amount on Coinbase.

You should take into a few things before you start using Coinbase. If you issue an automatic purchase order, you'll not be able to control the price at which the Bitcoins are purchased. The next thing you want to take note of is that Coinbase isn't a Bitcoin exchange. You're purchasing or selling your coins directly from that firm, which has to source them from another purchaser. This makes issues or delays when you're executing orders during a fast market move.

For those who want a traditional Bitcoin exchange, BitStamp might be a better option. BitStamp allows you to trade with other users and not the actual company; they only act as a middleman. Liquidating Bitcoins this way is much more profitable, and you can almost always find someone else to take your trade. The fees begin at half a percent and go all the way down to two-tenths of a percent if you trade over $150,000 worth of Bitcoins in thirty days.

Other Ways to Purchase

Exchanges aren't the only way you can obtain a Bitcoin. A popular way to purchase them offline is with Local Bitcoins. The website pairs you up with a potential seller or buyer. When you are purchasing Bitcoins, they are locked from the seller in an escrow account. The seller is only able to release them to the buyer. That way, if there is a dispute, you can file within twenty-four hours. When you are purchasing Bitcoins offline, remember to take the usual precautions you should when you're meeting a stranger. Meet during the day at a public place, and if you can, bring a friend with you.

Bitcoins are a hot item right now, and the investors and venture capital firms are thinking it's going to be here for the long-term. For those average person, there are many ways you can invest in and purchase Bitcoins.

Chapter Seven - Bitcoins for Business

Many businesses are asking themselves if they should be accepting Bitcoins, and the answer is yes! In this chapter, you'll learn why your company should accept Bitcoins, and you'll learn which countries are currently allowing Bitcoin to operate in them.

Why Companies Should Use Bitcoins

1. **A company doesn't have to be an expert in Bitcoins in order to start accepting them.**

Many people are attempting to grasp the idea of what a Bitcoin is, and you can spend anywhere from a day to a week reading about the concept in order to feel more comfortable using it. You shouldn't let that frighten you. There's no doubt that a steep learning curve, when it comes to understanding what a Bitcoin is and how it works, exists. Fortunately, companies such as BitPay.com and Coinbase.com help new users walk through the entire process of setting up and accepting Bitcoins for companies.

2. Accepting Bitcoins isn't going to make or break a company.

Less than one percent of the population uses Bitcoins if that. Therefore, unless your business is tied directly to Bitcoins as a whole, odds are you will see very little commerce that's tied directly to Bitcoins. This might sound like a reason you shouldn't accept Bitcoins, but keep in mind, the users of Bitcoins is growing every day, and while the amount of users right now might be small, the amount of users in the future could be much larger. However, for today, realize that this won't save a dying business, but it won't send your business into a downward spiral, either.

3. Bitcoins are very successful in the non-profit industry.

Are you someone who runs a non-profit, or does your business do business with local charities? Bitcoins are a great way to raise awareness for non-profits, and they're used to help fund donations across the globe. WikiLinks has used Bitcoins in order to keep their public donations alive.

4. Your business isn't going to be exposed to price volatility.

There's no doubt that if you have followed Bitcoin for over the past couple of years, the most discussed topic is whether the price is relative to the dollar. From an investment viewpoint, Bitcoin isn't the best investment. It's not rare to see the price of the Bitcoin go up or down twenty percent in just one day. It's for this reason alone that business owners are afraid of Bitcoin. If you sell a service or a good for a hundred dollars, as a business owner, you want to make sure you receive that one hundred dollars.

The thought of accepting payment in Bitcoin and discovering that the following day it's only worth half its value is a legitimate fear. Fortunately, this issue is solved easily. Going back to those companies that were mentioned before, Coinbase and BitPay, these companies both allow you to set a process to convert Bitcoins to dollars instantly. This means that the moment you receive a payment in Bitcoin, the software converts that Bitcoin into dollars. So when a payment of a hundred dollars in Bitcoins is accepted, you will receive those one hundred dollars, no matter what the price fluctuation is.

5. **Adding Bitcoins helps you reconnect with your past or existing clients or customers.**

Other than the functionality of what Bitcoins are able to do for your business, adding them as a payment method provides you with an opportunity to connect with previous customers and clients. An email blast is an excellent way to share your business's present vision and where you see it going in the future.

6. **Adding Bitcoins provides you with the opportunity to become an industry leader.**

Most businesses didn't start using social media because they saw a competitive advantage in the beginning stages. They added Facebook and Twitter to their repertoire because everyone else was using them, too. Those are not the businesses who are industry leaders.

Bitcoin gives you the opportunity to become an industry leader in your respective field of business. Ten years from now, most businesses are probably going to be accepting Bitcoins. There will always be those who are old school and determined to do it the way it's always been done, but most are going to see the benefits of using Bitcoins years from now.

7. **Bitcoin helps fuel media coverage and raise brand awareness for your business.**

Even if your industry doesn't seem like it would benefit from using new technology, you'd be surprised the amount of exposure you'd receive. You can list your business in new local directories to let people know you're accepting Bitcoins. Local news outlets are a great way to connect with potential clients and customers because Bitcoins is one of the leading buzzwords now, so news channels are always looking for a new angle to report on.

8. Accepting Bitcoins can lower your transaction fees.

One of the easiest benefits you'll get is the amount of money you could save by switching to using Bitcoins. Aside from them being easy to use and quick, the transaction fees are one of the leading reasons businesses are making the switch right now. Unlike the traditional methods used for paying, such as PayPal or credit cards, Bitcoin can make transactions simple and quick without the need for transactions fees.

For businesses with an e-commerce presence, this is a pretty simple decision to make. For those who are running small brick and mortar company, it might be a little less of an advantage. However, with credit card fees going as high as three percent and PayPal capping out at six percent, it's easy to see why a company would enjoy a zero percent transaction fee. Companies can take this a little further and pass the savings onto their customers or clients by providing them with discounts when they purchase a service or item with Bitcoin.

9. You can help grow your business with the support of the Bitcoin community.

The disadvantages versus the advantages of using Bitcoin are still not very clear. One thing that is a given, though, is that Bitcoin users love supporting their community. There're a large number of enthusiasts out there who are willing to go out of their way to support a Bitcoin-friendly business.

There're thousands of Bitcoin enthusiasts around the world who are willing and eager to spend this currency, and up until now, their options were limited.

10. Accepting Bitcoins empowers your clients and customers.

Many companies make the mistake of wondering what's in it for them when they should be wondering what's in it for their customers. If you take a moment and look at the big picture, all Bitcoin has done is add another option for customers to pay with. Today, more than ever, businesses in each industry are attempting to stand out by providing their customers with a unique experience. One way to customize your business is to let your customers choose the way they want to pay for your goods and services. Accepting Bitcoin most likely won't be the reason someone chooses to do business with your company, but having Bitcoin as an option only adds to the reasons why they might choose you.

Countries that Accept Bitcoin

Due to Bitcoins being able to be used anonymously between account holders, it has become attractive to criminal operations. However, many countries have made regulations and rules that protect against this as much as they can. Yet, this element to Bitcoin has made the currency a little unsavory to some countries; therefore, there are countries who accept Bitcoin and others who do not.

Let's look at the countries who accept Bitcoin in this section.

The United States

Generally, the United States has taken a more positive approach to the new currency. At the same time, several agencies are working to prevent or reduce the use of Bitcoin for illegal activity. Prominent business, such as Dish Network and Amazon, will accept Bitcoin as payment. The digital currency has made its way into the United States derivatives market, too.

The Department of Treasury's Financial Crimes Enforcement Network has issued guidance on Bitcoin starting in 2013. They have defined Bitcoin not as a currency, but as a money service business. This puts it under the Bank Secrecy Act, which requires payment processors and exchanges to adhere to certain responsibilities, such as registration, reporting, and record keeping. Bitcoin has been categorized as property for taxation purposes, meaning it must be reported to the IRS.

Canada

Like the United States, Canada has a Bitcoin-friendly view, but they ensure that the currency isn't used for money laundering. The Canada Revenue Agency, CRA, views Bitcoin as a commodity. This means the transactions are viewed as being barter transactions, and the income that is generated from them is considered a business income. The taxation depends on whether the individual has a purchasing-selling business or is only investing in Bitcoins.

Canada considers a Bitcoin exchange to be a money service business. This ensures Bitcoin exchanges are under the anti-money laundering laws. Exchanges have to register with the Financial Transactions and Reports Analysis Centre, report suspicious transactions, keep certain records, and abide by compliance plans. The government has assigned the responsibility to the Senate Banking Committee with conscripting the rules and regulations for legislation of virtual currencies.

Australia

The Australian Taxation Office classifies Bitcoin transactions as a barter arrangement that is subject to the corresponding taxes depending on the use and the user.

The European Union

While the European Union has tracked the progress of cryptocurrencies, they have not issued an official decision on legality, regulation, or acceptance. In the absence of a central guidance, those in European Union countries have created their own Bitcoin stance. A few nations allow Bitcoins while others issue warnings or are undecided on the subject.

In Finland, the CBT has added a value-added tax exempt status to Bitcoin by classifying it as a financial service. It is treated as a commodity rather than a currency. The Federal Public Service Finance in Belgium has made it exempt from VAT.

Countries that Do Not Accept Bitcoins

Bitcoin is welcome in many areas of the world, but there are some who are wary of Bitcoins. Amongst those countries are Iceland, Vietnam, Bolivia, Kyrgyzstan, Ecuador, Russia, and China.

Chapter Eight - Bitcoins for Regular Non-Technical Users

For those who are of the non-technical variety, Bitcoin can still be a viable option for paying for goods and services. You don't have to be a technical genius to join in on the Bitcoin revolution.

So how can you use Bitcoins?

1. **Charity and Tipping**

One of the most rewarding ways to spend your Bitcoins is to give it away. Use them to tip blog post and article writers with just a simple click of a button or donate to a number of different charities. You can purchase Reddit Gold with Bitcoins, and give it out as gratitude to users who post your favorite articles.

You can send and receive tips with charitable donations or Changetip.

You can use your personal payment pages to begin accepting Bitcoin immediately.

2. Household Items

With a million products for sale, all available in Bitcoins, overstock.com allows you to purchase just about anything you need for your home.

3. Gift Cards

Stores such as BestBuy and Amazon accept Bitcoins on their site, but some enterprising individuals have found a workaround for spending their Bitcoin. Use them to purchase gift cards from places such as Gyft or eGifter, and then redeem them at hundreds of other popular retailers across the internet.

4. Video Games

Companies such as Green Man Gaming and Microsoft have begun offering games and other apps in exchange for Bitcoins. Others, such as Minecraft, are using the network to power their in-game currency, and making money at it!

5. Food

You can find apps on Android and IOS that allow you to find restaurants and coffee shops that accept Bitcoins. In fact, some of them only accept Bitcoins!

6. Travel

On Expedia, you can pay for a hotel with Bitcoins. You can book a flight on CheapAir, or you can take a cruise with Ships and Trips Travel. In fact, car dealerships are starting to get in on the game. While paying for gas with Bitcoins hasn't come to life yet, there are people working on machines that will allow it.

So how do you pay with Bitcoin?

1. **Pay with a Coinbase wallet.**

If you're doing business with a merchant who uses Coinbase to receive Bitcoin disbursements and you have an account that is funded, then you can complete the checkout by signing into your account and confirming your order. Once you've confirmed the order, the process is completed, and the merchant is notified of your payment.

2. **QR Codes**

A QR code represents a Bitcoin address and a payment account, so most Bitcoin processors will accept them. They make it easy to pay from your Bitcoin wallet app on a smartphone. Just scan the QR code and it'll fill in the receiver's Bitcoin address and the amount that is requested. Once you send it, it's complete. This is good if you don't have a Coinbase account, or you want to pay from a different wallet.

3. **Pay to an address.**

If you're not able to scan a QR code or the merchant provides a Bitcoin address only, you can manually enter this into your Bitcoin wallet software. To pay an address, you'll need two pieces of information – the Bitcoin address of the recipient, and the amount of the Bitcoin you're sending.

Both of these are going to be displayed on the payment page as you check out, but some are going to leave the amount up to you in the case of a donation or a more flexible payment model.

With the amount and address, just enter them into the send form of the wallet and submit.

If the merchant uses Coinbase, shortly after you send your payment, the checkout page is going to update in order to show that the funds were received. The purchase is then marked as finished. Note that for another payment processor or direct payments without using a processor, the process can be a little different.

Chapter Nine - Bitcoin Wallets

There are a few different ways you can use Bitcoin, and so there are a few different types of wallets you can have. There are online Bitcoin wallets, which are able to be accessed on the internet anywhere you have access. Then there are hardware wallets, which are physical devices that are designed to secure your Bitcoins. There are software wallets, which are applications you download to your computer, phone, or tablet. Then there are paper wallets, which are private keys that are printed from your offline computer.

By the end of this chapter, you'll understand the different types of wallet, and have a better idea about which one is right for you. Here are some things you might want to consider as you're choosing the type of wallet you want to use.

- Are you always on the go? If you're making payments in person and you're not online, then a mobile wallet might be a better option for you.

- Do you make a lot of payments during the day? If you need to make a lot of payments throughout the day, then it might be better to keep your funds in a wallet that's easily accessible and easy to use. Mobile wallets and desktop ones are both good ideas.
- Are you handling large amounts? If you're handling a lot of Bitcoins, then you want a secure wallet. A hardware wallet and a secure offline wallet, such as Armory, is a good option.
- Do you use combinations? If you use a mobile wallet as the checking out account, and you use a hardware or a secure offline wallet as a savings account, then you want to mix and match different types of wallets to provide you with accessibility and the most security.

Universal Wallets

Copay is a wallet that was created by Bitpay, and it's available on Android, iOS, Windows, Mac OS X, and Linux. Because it's available on numerous different platforms, it's easy for you to use the same account or wallet across numerous devices.

It's a clean, simple user interface that makes it a good choice for those who are new to Bitcoin. It's also a good option for a business because it has shared account features, which require a specific amount of operators to sign a transaction. For example, two co-founders would be able to make a 2 of 2 wallet where both were needed to sign off on a transaction.

Hardware Wallets

These are small computers or a smartcard that's built with the single purpose of creating Bitcoin private keys offline. Hardware wallets will securely sign a transaction in the same offline environment.

Some ones to consider are:

- **Ledger Nano –** This is a smartcard based hardware wallet. The private key is produced and signed offline in the smartcard's protected environment. It's setup using the Chrome Application. A random, twenty-four-word seed is created when it's setup, and you back it up offline by writing it down on a piece of paper. In case of damage, theft, or loss, the entire wallet is able to be recreated with the seed. Your selected PIN code is assigned to the device to protect against hacking or physical theft.

- **Trezor** – This hardware wallet is different from the Ledger Nano because it's a tiny computer instead of a smartcard. The private key is still created offline. It generated a twenty-four-word seed when it's started up, and it has its own built-in screen where your seed code is displayed and copied down when it's backed up. Because it's an offline device, it offers you extra security because the seed isn't displayed on a computer that's online. You can use an additional passcode to the twenty-four-word seed. This provides you with extra security because anyone who finds someone else's twenty-four-word seed is free to get into their funds. If the optional pass key is added, then a hacker still can't access the funds without the pass code and the seed combination. If the pass code is forgotten, you can't recover it, so make sure you choose something you can remember!
- **Opendime** – The first Bitcoin bearer bond or Bitcoin stick, Opendime is a USB stick that lets you spend Bitcoin as if you were spending cash. You can pass it along numerous times. You can connect it to any USB to check the balance. You can unseal it anytime to spend Bitcoins online. It acts like a ready-only USB flash drive and works with any phone, laptop, or computer. A QR code or text file inside contains the Bitcoin address and support. The private key is created inside the device, and not even you know it!

Online Bitcoin Wallets

Online wallets, also known as web wallets, store the private key online. They can be accessed with a user-set password.

- **GreenAddress** – This is a multi-signature wallet with applications for iOS, Chrome, and Android.
- **SpectroCoin** – This is a single solution for Bitcoin. Services offered include everything from exchange to e-wallets.

Mobile Wallets for Android

- **breadwallet** – This began as the most popular wallet for the iPhone, and it's available on Android devices now. This easy-to-use and simple security application make it a great app to begin with for those who are new to Bitcoin.
- **Mycelium** – This is a favorite program amongst those who are familiar with Bitcoin. It's an HD wallet that has numerous different features, both simple and advanced, such as watch-only accounts, Tor, and cold storage spending.
- **Bitcoin Wallet** – This program was the first one for Android. It's easy to backup, simple to use, and connects right to the Bitcoin network using SPV.

Mobile Wallets for iOS

- **Copay** – Available in the App Store, Copay is one of the more popular, easy to use apps for Bitcoins.
- **Airbitz** – This is another app that's available on the App Store with great reviews.

Desktop Wallets

These wallets are software wallets that you can download and install on your desktop or laptop. The desktop wallets are available on Windows, Mac, and Linux.

- **Armory** – This is the most secure, mature and full-featured Bitcoin wallet, but it's intimidating for users who are not technologically savvy. Whether you're someone who's storing a thousand dollars, or you're an institute storing a million dollars, this is the most secure option out there. Users are in complete

control of their Bitcoins and their private keys, and they can setup secure, offline-signing processes in armory.
- **Bitcoin Core** – This is the official Bitcoin wallet and client, but it's not used by many because of the slow speeds and the lack of features. However, it's a full node, which means it helps transmit and verify other Bitcoin transactions across the network, and it stores a copy of the blockchain. This offers you better privacy because it doesn't have to rely on information from an external server or another peer in the network. It's routed through Tor and is considered one of the best ways to use Bitcoin securely.
- **Electrum** – This is the most popular desktop wallet because of its speed and usability. It can be used as cold storage if you have an extra desktop that can be used offline. In addition, it offers other features, such as connection to Tor, integrating with hardware wallets, and multi-signature wallets.

Paper Wallets

These are the standard method of cold storage, at least, before the hardware wallets were created. They are private keys that are printed out on a piece of paper and stored wherever you like. If they are created and printed with a secure, offline computer, they are secure cold storage that no one can access.

The main issue with paper wallets is it's not convenient to make and print a net wallet every time you send funds to cold storage. Yet, it's possible to bulk print your paper wallets to save you time and eliminate the address reuse.

Chapter Ten - Important Warnings about Bitcoins

While Bitcoins are the future of currency, there are some things you want to consider before you get into using them. This chapter is not meant to frighten you away from using Bitcoins but to educate you about the possible pitfalls. Once you're educated, you can protect yourself against them.

1. **They're not widely accepted yet.**

They are still only accepted by a small minority of online merchants; however, they are being accepted by some of the larger merchants, such as Amazon. This makes it not feasible to rely on them entirely as a currency yet. There's a possibility that governments could force merchants to stop using Bitcoins to ensure the user's transactions are able to be traced.

2. **You can lose a wallet.**

If your hard drive crashes or a virus corrupts your data, then your Bitcoins have been lost. There's nothing you can do to recover them. It's as if you've burned paper money. These coins will be orphaned in the system forever. This can bankrupt wealthy Bitcoin investors in just seconds with no way to recover. The coins the investor owned will be permanently lost.

3. **The value of Bitcoins changes constantly.**

The value of Bitcoins is always changing according to the demand. One Bitcoin was valued at $9.90 on an exchange site on June 2nd, 2011. It was valued at less than $1 in just six months. This constant changing of the value of Bitcoins can cause Bitcoin-accepting sites to change their prices all the time. It'll also cause a lot of confusion if you need to refund a product. For example, a t-shirt you originally purchased for one Bitcoin could be valued at two and a half Bitcoins the following week when you return it. This can cause some confusion and issues.

4. **There is no buyer protection.**

When items are purchased using Bitcoins, and the seller doesn't deliver on the sale, nothing is able to be done to reverse a transaction. This problem is solvable by using a third-party escrow service, such as ClearCoin, but these are assuming the role of a bank, which could cause Bitcoin to turn out to be more like a traditional currency.

5. **There's a risk of unidentified technical defects.**

The system could have unexploited flaws so far that no one knows. Because this is still a new structure, if Bitcoins were accepted extensively and someone were to find a flaw, then it could give a lot of wealth to the one exploiting the system and the expense of destroying the economy.

6. **Bitcoin has built-in deflation.**

Because the number of Bitcoins that can be found is capped at twenty-one million, this will cause deflation. Every Bitcoin will be worth more and more as the total number begins to max out. This system is designed to reward only those who adopted the system early on. Because it will be valued with every passing day, the question of when to spend will become important. This could cause a spending surge that will cause the Bitcoin economy to fluctuate unpredictably and rapidly.

7. There's no physical form.

Because Bitcoins are virtual and not physical, they cannot be used in a physical store. They would always have to be converted to another currency. Cards with the Bitcoin wallet information stored in them will need to be created, but there's no consensus on a specific system. Because there would be numerous competitors, merchants might find it not profitable to upkeep all Bitcoin cards, and therefore, users would be required to exchange their Bitcoins into cash anyway.

8. There's no valuation guarantee.

There is no central authority that governs Bitcoins, which means no one is able to guarantee a minimum valuation. If a large group decides to dump Bitcoins and leave the system, then its valuation is going to decrease greatly, which will hurt the users greatly. The decentralized nature is both a blessing and a curse.

> Again, just because there are pitfalls to the system doesn't mean you shouldn't invest now or get involved. Remember, those who get into the system early on are the ones who will be rewarded the most.

Chapter Eleven - Short Guide on Other Cryptocurrencies

Not only has Bitcoin been a leader in the cryptocurrency industry, but it's been paving the way for new cryptocurrencies to come about. The currencies inspired by Bitcoin are known as altcoins, and they have tried to represent themselves as being a better or improved version of the original Bitcoin. While some of them are easier to obtain than Bitcoin, there are some tradeoffs, such as a great peril brought on by reduced liquidity, value retention, and acceptance. Let's look at some of the other cryptocurrencies out there.

#1 Litecoin

Launched in 2011, Litecoin was amongst the first cryptocurrencies out there after Bitcoin and is often referred to as the silver to Bitcoin's gold. It was made by Charlie Lee, an MIT student, and former Google employee. It was based on the open source worldwide payment system that's not controlled by a dominant power and uses 'scrypt' as the evidence of work, which is able to be decoded with the help of CPUs and consumer grade.

While it's like Bitcoin in numerous ways, it has a faster block creation rate and offers a quicker transaction validation. Other than developers, there're a number of merchants who are accepting Litecoin.

#2 Ethereum

Created in 2015, this cryptocurrency is a distributed software system that lets Smart Contracts and Distributed Applications to be created and utilized without downtime, control, fraud, or interference from a third party. In 2014, it had launched a presale for either that had received an overwhelmingly positive response.

The applications on this system are run on the platform-specific cryptographic token, known as ether. It's like a vehicle for moving around on the platform, and it's sought my numerous developers who are hoping to create and run applications inside the platform. According to the founders, it can be used to decentralize, codify, trade, and secure just about anything.

After the attack on the DAO in 2016, it was split into Ethereum Classic and Ethereum. Etherum is second in market capitalization after Bitcoin at $4.46 billion.

#3 Zcash

At the end of 2016, Zcash was launched. It's an open-source and decentralized cryptocurrency that looks rather promising. Zcash defines itself as the https of http. It offers selective transparency of transactions and privacy. Therefore, like https, it claims to provide the users with extra privacy and security where all transactions are recorded and published on the blockchain, but the details (recipient, sender, and the amount) are all private.

This platform offers its users the choice of a shielded transactions, which allows for content to be encrypted with advanced cryptographic techniques or zero-knowledge proof constructions known as zk-SNARK developed by the team.

#4 Dash

Originally known as Darkcoin, Dash is a secretive version of Bitcoin. It offers more privacy and works on a distributed mastercode system that creates virtually untraceable transactions. Dash was launched in January of 2014 and experienced an increase in following in a short amount of time. This cryptocurrency was made and developed by Evan Duffield, and it can be mined with a GPU or CPU. In March of 2015, it was rebranded as Dash, which stands for Digital Cash and uses the ticker DASH. The change in company name didn't modify any of its features, such as InstantX and Darksend.

#5 Ripple

This is a real-time global settlement network that offers its users certain, instant and low-cost international payments. It allows banks to settle cross-border payments immediately, with transparency and lower costs. Ripple was released in 2012 and has a market capitalization of $1.26 billion.

Its consensus ledger, which is the method it uses for conformation, doesn't need mining, a feature that is different from many altcoins and Bitcoins. Due to its structure not requiring mining, it reduces the usage of computing power and minimizes the network latency. The company's founder believes that distributing value is a powerful way to incentivize behaviors, and therefore, they plan to distribute XRP primarily through business developmental deals, retailing XRP to official purchasers interested in investing, and incentives to liquidity providers.

#6 Monero

This cryptocurrency is a private, secure, and untraceable currency. It's an open-source currency that was released in April of 2014, and it soon spiked a large interest amongst the cryptocurrency enthusiasts. The development of Monero is a donation-based and community-driven platform. It has been launched with the strong focus on scalability and decentralization. It enables a completely private transaction using a technique known as ring signatures. With this method, there is a group of cryptocurrency signatures including one real participant, but since they all look valid, the real one is not isolated.

Bitcoin is the pack leader of cryptocurrencies, but if you feel you don't want to get into the bigger pool, then you might want to think about investing in one of the other cryptocurrencies out there.

Conclusion

Despite Bitcoin's volatility, the cryptocurrency is still going strong because of the community that has been built around its platform. While it's difficult to mine Bitcoins as an individual, you can join a mining group in order to obtain some of this cryptocurrency, and if you want to get in the game, now is the time! You might not become a millionaire off Bitcoin immediately, but it could be a great investment for the future. Who knows, a Bitcoin might be worth millions of dollars by the time you retire.

Just remember, be smart about where you store your Bitcoins, and make sure you backup your files and keep your computer protected. Treat your Bitcoins as if they were cash because they essentially are.

I hope you enjoyed reading this book about Bitcoins. If you did, please leave a review at your online retailer's website.

Thank you for reading, and don't forget to check out the bonus at the end of this book!

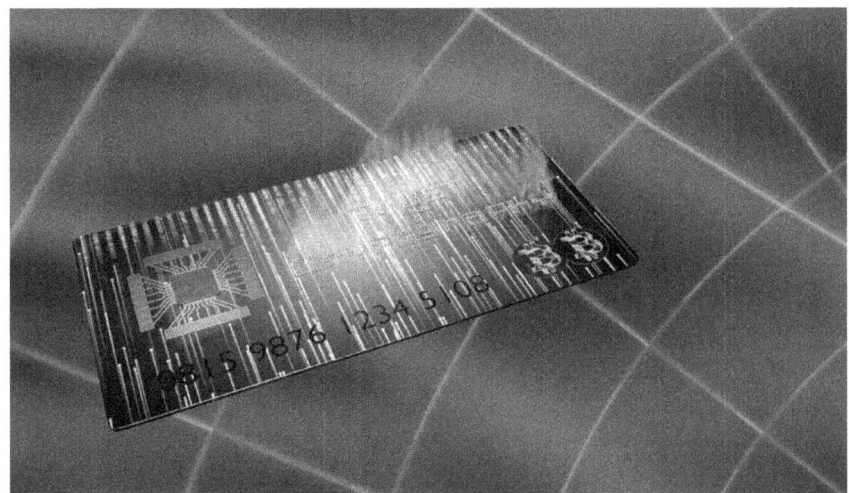

Bonus: Fun Facts about Bitcoins

1. **The Bitcoin creator, Satoshi Nakamoto, is still not known.**

The alias, Satoshi Nakamoto, was the designation used by the individual or individuals who created Bitcoin, but there's still uncertainty about who really made this system. Over the years, a few different people have been linked to the alias, including Nick Szabo, Dorian Nakamoto, Craig Steven Wright, Hal Finney, and many others. Some people consider the alias to be a team rather than just one person. As of May 2017, the alias is believed to own around one million Bitcoins, with the net worth being more than $2 billion.

2. **Bitcoins are limited.**

You might've heard about the mining process, but there isn't an infinite number of Bitcoins. A pre-defined schedule has limited the number of this commodity. They're slowing approaching the total of 21 million, and the mining process gets harder every day.

3. **It's impossible to know the receiver and sender details.**

The Bitcoin addresses are a long string of numbers and letters. With that address, it's impossible to figure out who is receiving the Bitcoins and who is sending them. This is most likely why most of the illegal transactions are being carried out with Bitcoins. To protect their privacy even further, most wallet platforms allocate the consumers with an ID, which is used as a username.

4. **Pizza was the first thing that was purchased with Bitcoin.**

After the Bitcoin transaction happened between Hal Finney and Satoshi in 2009, the first recorded purchase was a pizza for $25. 10,000 Bitcoins were spent for this pizza.

5. **The Bitcoin network is more powerful than supercomputers.**

According to experts, the Bitcoin network has a computing power of 2,046,364 Pflops/s. If you combine the computing power of about five hundred of the most powerful computers out there, you'll get around 274 Pflop/s.

6. **Bitcoin was in outer space.**

Genesis Mining, in 2016, a Bitcoin cloud mining provider, sent Bitcoin into space. This was done with a Bitcoin paper wallet and a 3D Bitcoin model, which were both tied to a weather balloon. The entire journey was recorded with a GoPro focused on the wallet and model. Once the weather balloon reached 20 kilometers, the ground team made the transaction to a paper wallet. Another allocation was completed once it achieved the maximum altitude of 34 kms.

7. **Bitcoin transfers are irreversible.**

Transactions of Bitcoins are not able to be reversed. Unlike the popular platforms like PayPal, you don't get a second chance when you make a transaction. When it's sent, it's sent.

8. **The FBI has one of the biggest Bitcoin wallets.**

When the operations of Silk Road were shut down, the FBI seized the owners' assets. In this process, the FBI became one of the wealthiest Bitcoin owners in the world. A report from Wired magazine claims the FBI controls around $120 million worth of Bitcoins.

9. Losing a Bitcoin wallet means you've lost the Bitcoins forever.

Once the Bitcoins are lost, they can never be retrieved. Wallets are highly secured for this reason. Once someone steals them, no one can ever find them again.

10. Bitcoins are highly volatile.

Since their launch, in the past ten years, Bitcoin has become one of the most imperative phenomena in the world. Its price has reached thousands of dollars for a single Bitcoin. However, the price fluctuates all the time, and it has remained volatile. Predictions have been made that they might fall in the future if they follow the current path.

Copyright 2017
Published in the United States by Richard Brana / © Richard Brana-
All rights Reserved. No part of this publication or the information in it may be quoted from or reproduced in any form by means such as printing, scanning, photocopying or otherwise without prior written permission of the copyright holder.
Disclaimer and Terms of Use: Effort has been made to ensure that the information in this book is accurate and complete, however, the author and the publisher do not warrant the accuracy of the information, text and graphics contained within the book due to the rapidly changing nature of science, research, known and unknown facts and internet. The Author and the publisher do not hold any responsibility for errors, omissions or contrary interpretation of the subject matter herein. This book is presented solely for motivational and informational purposes only.

www.ingramcontent.com/pod-product-compliance
Lightning Source LLC
Chambersburg PA
CBHW050023230526
45470CB00003B/1099